THE OIL OF EXCELLENCE

THE OIL OF EXCELLENCE

How to Move Beyond Average
and Mediocrity in the Pursuit of Destiny

Dr. John A. Tetsola

The Oil of Excellence

How to Move Beyond Average and Mediocrity in the Pursuit of Destiny

ISBN 1-929620-09-8

TABLE OF CONTENTS

CHAPTER I

UNDERSTANDING THE SPIRIT OF EXCELLENCE

[A Psalm of David] LORD, I cry unto thee: make haste unto me; give ear unto my voice, when I cry unto thee.

Let my prayer be set forth before thee [as] incense; [and] the lifting up of my hands [as] the evening sacrifice.

Set a watch, O LORD, before my mouth; keep the door of my lips.

Incline not my heart to [any] evil thing, to practise wicked works with men that work iniquity: and let me not eat of their dainties.

Let the righteous smite me; [it shall be] a kindness:

and let him reprove me; [it shall be] an excellent oil,

[which] shall not break my head: for yet my prayer

also [shall be] in their calamities.

Psalms 141:1-4 KJV

Psalm 141 begins with David offering fervent prayers to the LORD GOD. Perhaps he was in the temple during the evening sacrifice. As the sweet fragrance of the incense filled the temple, David lifts his hands and asks God to allow his prayers to ascend to His throne in heaven as sweetly as the cloud of incense.

David goes on to ask God to assist him in keeping his mouth shut in verse 3. Even in the sanctuary we can see things to talk about. David sees the value in focusing on God, and not speaking about what he sees. Because the tongue is the hardest thing to tame in the human anatomy, David pleads for divine assistance.

He's going for the gold here and understands that only with God's help will he be able to attain that place of excellence in God for which David strives.

In verse 5, while ruminating on how good things can be painful at times, the Psalmist draws the analogy between being corrected by one who is righteous to the extraction process of "excellent" oil.

> **Let the righteous smite me; it shall be a kindness: and let him reprove me; it shall be an excellent oil, which shall not break my head: for yet my prayer also shall be in their calamities.**

> **Psalms 141:5 (KJV)**

Here, the Psalmist David shares with us his observations on the eternal value or end result of being "hammered"— like iron in the production of a mighty sword — by the righteous. Impurities or slag must be worked out of the iron ore by force. The metal had to be heated and hammered, heated and hammered, until a bonding occurred and two pieces become one sword.

This hammering of reproof or correction by the righteous is facilitated by the knowledge that it brings forth an oil that is excellent. Through the Holy Spirit, David sees the significant benefits of chastisement or reproof, no matter how unpleasant, and determines not to refuse it. David draws an analogy between the correction or reproof of a righteous man and "excellent" oil.

This oil will bring change, beginning with my head, which speaks of headship and authority. And because I am not refusing it, it will flow down my entire body, which speaks of ministry and anything that we are connected to. The oil of excellence on a leader is reflected in his ministry, his family, and all that is connected to him or all that his hand finds to do. This oil will not kill you, but it will promote and elevate you, and positively change you and your ministry for good. When I am changed or converted, then I can pray for my enemies in their evil day, instead of killing them.

This analogy implies there is an oil that is not excellent. There is a negative anointing that flows through contact with wicked and ungodly individuals. Perhaps this is what the Apostle Paul wrote about in 1 Corinthians 15:33, when he warned Corinthian believers that "evil communications corrupt good manners."

The Excellent Name

To the chief Musician upon Gittith, A Psalm of David. O LORD our Lord, how excellent is thy name in all the earth! who hast set thy glory above the heavens.

Psalms 8:1 (KJV)

God's name is excellent. His personality, character, and His temperament are excellent. His actions are all excellent. When He created man, He created man with His mind. The name of a person in the Bible denotes their character, personality, nature, temperament, authority and everything about that person. Jacob, in the Scripture, meant cheater, heel grabber, deceiver, manipulator and liar. And he lived the meaning of his name through his personality, temperament, and character. The name of Jesus portrays the character, personality, authority, nature and temperament of God. That is why, as Christians, we must be very careful about the names we give our children. The name you give your child will sometimes denote the manifestations of their character, personality, nature and the authority they will walk in after they are born again. In Ephesians 5:1, Paul says let us be imitators of God. That means, we must be a people of excellence. Excellence is a lifestyle. It is the lifestyle of the kingdom. Excellence is one of the keys of promotion in life and in ministry. It will unlock doors for you everywhere you go.

In history, the word "excellence" was used as a title of honor. It is derived from the word "excel," which means "to go beyond average." The spirit of excellence is the ability to go beyond average. It is going beyond what others expect. The spirit of excellence says while everyone else works from 9:00 a.m. to 5:00 p.m., I will work from 9:00 a.m. until 7:00 p.m. It is always determining to go beyond the norm. That is a key that brings about promotion in our lives. The ability to go beyond average will promote you in the land of average and mediocre. The word "excellence" in Hebrew means "preeminent" or "outstanding." When you walk in integrity, God will always cause you to walk in excellence.

Andre Maurois said these words, "If you create an act, you create a habit. If you create a habit, you create a character. If you create a character, you create a destiny." D.L. Moody said "If I take care of my character, my reputation will take care of itself," and Aristotle said, "To enjoy the things we ought, and to hate the things we ought, has the greatest bearing on excellence of character." Character is like a tree, and reputation and excellence are like its shadow. The shadow is what we think of it, but only the tree has the substance of reality.

The Challenge To Go Higher

God wants to challenge us to a high standard of excellence in everything that we do. Do the best you can right where you are. Let it be the highest level of excellence, whatever the standard of living, or whatever the standard of spirituality to which God has brought you. You may not be able to compete with a neighbor, but you can be excellent where you are with what you have. Don't live a mediocre, average life. Live with direction. Live a life that has been programmed and scripted by God. Live by deliberate principles of success. It will lead you to an ultimate destination, a goal that finishes and fulfills God's purpose for your life. You can do well in a lot of things God never inspired. That is not success.

It pleased Darius to set over the kingdom an hundred and twenty princes, which should be over the whole kingdom;

And over these three presidents; of whom Daniel was first: that the princes might give accounts unto them, and the king should have no damage.

Then this Daniel was preferred above the presidents and princes, because an excellent spirit was in him; and the king thought to set him over the whole realm.

Daniel 6:1-3 (KJV)

Daniel was a man who walked and operated in the oil of excellence. He was outstanding and preeminent. Daniel so walked in excellence that he stood out from the others. Daniel was faithful to his God and was willing to go beyond average which caused him to stand out. Your faithfulness to God will produce the spirit of excellence. Faithfulness is a virtue that will cause a person to stand out from the crowd and to receive God's undivided attention.

The Solomon and Sheba Encounter

And when the queen of Sheba heard of the fame of Solomon, she came to prove Solomon with hard questions at Jerusalem, with a very great company, and camels that bare spices, and gold in abundance, and precious stones: and when she was come to Solomon, she communed with him of all that was in her heart.

And Solomon told her all her questions: and there was nothing hid from Solomon which he told her not.

And when the queen of Sheba had seen the wisdom of Solomon, and the house that he had built,

And the meat of his table, and the sitting of his servants, and the attendance of his ministers, and their apparel; his cupbearers also, and their apparel; and his ascent by which he went up into the house of the LORD; there was no more spirit in her.

And she said to the king, It was a true report which
I heard in mine own land of thine acts, and of thy
wisdom:

Howbeit I believed not their words, until I came,
and mine eyes had seen it: and, behold, the one half
of the greatness of thy wisdom was not told me: for
thou exceedest the fame that I heard.

Happy are thy men, and happy are these thy
servants, which stand continually before thee, and
hear thy wisdom.

Blessed be the LORD thy God, which delighted in
thee to set thee on his throne, to be king for the
LORD thy God: because thy God loved Israel, to
establish them for ever, therefore made he thee king
over them, to do judgment and justice.

And she gave the king an hundred and twenty talents of gold, and of spices great abundance, and precious stones: neither was there any such spice as the queen of Sheba gave king Solomon.

And the servants also of Huram, and the servants of Solomon, which brought gold from Ophir, brought algum trees and precious stones.

And the king made of the algum trees terraces to the house of the LORD, and to the king's palace, and harps and psalteries for singers: and there were none such seen before in the land of Judah.

And king Solomon gave to the queen of Sheba all her desire, whatsoever she asked, beside that which she had brought unto the king. So she turned, and went away to her own land, she and her servants.

2 Chronicles 9:1-12 (KJV)

Look at the story of the encounter of King Solomon with Queen Sheba. She heard of the fame of Solomon and she came to get in on his ministry. She prepared questions to ask Solomon because she had heard that he was a very wise man. But when she met Solomon, she met a man not only full of wisdom, but a man with the spirit of excellence flowing in his ministry and life. We need excellence in our lives and ministries because it keeps the devil out.

Solomon was able to answer all of Queen Sheba's questions. She came with great authority and power, but because of Solomon's character, there was no more spirit in her. This was a woman who came with an intention and purpose to critique Solomon's ministry, but because Solomon walked in excellence the power of excellence diffused her power and took her breath away.

She noticed that Solomon's servants and workers were very alert. She noticed the servants' apparel. She saw the size of Solomon's men. She saw how happy they were in serving Solomon. This alarmed Queen Sheba. She marveled at his ministry of helps. She marveled at the attendance. She saw the oil of excellence upon these men and her breath was taken away. That is what happens when an individual or a ministry walks in excellence. It will cause the enemy to submit and give to you against his will. The oil of excellence upon a believer, a church or a ministry is powerful enough to destroy the intentions and assignments of the wicked one.

CHAPTER II

THE VALUE OF EXCELLENCE

Excellence is not an event. It is a discipline and an attitude. You choose an attitude. You choose excellence. It is not based on race, money, or whether or not you have a good mom and dad. It is a choice. Excellence should be our goal as Christians, if we are ever going to experience promotion. The first step to achieve and grow in excellence is to put a high value on excellence. What you do not value, you will not pursue. Let the pursuit of excellence become worthwhile to you. When you value something, you ascribe worth to it. Value is the very key in us to unlock the vault of blessings, favor and anointing in a thing, in a place, and in a person. You will only pursue that which you value. You will only receive from that which you value. And you will only give to that which you value. Our value for a thing determines how well and eagerly we pursue that thing. Value will create a hunger where there is none. For you to walk in the spirit of excellence in your life, family and ministry, you must first value the need for excellence.

The word "worship" is a derivation of the word "worthship" which means, what I do toward my God that costs me something. The value of that cost is worship. For example, the gasoline your car burns to get to church is worship. The meal you went without, and the time you spent on the freeway is worship.

Something you sacrifice in your life to put God first is worship, because it shows its worth and its value in your life. Whenever you look for and cherish the path of least resistance in life, you are avoiding worship. Out of every struggle, attack and trial in your life, God is constantly giving you an opportunity to worship Him. Worship involves cost. When you are offering something that does not cost you anything, that does not inconvenience you, then you are not worshiping God. So put value on excellence. Put value on going beyond average in your life.

The Comparison Between Success and Excellence

There is a difference between success and a lifestyle of excellence.

a) Success bases our worth on a comparison to others, but excellence gauges our value by measuring us against our own potential.

b) Success grants its reward to the few, yet it is the dream of many. Excellence is available to all, yet it is accepted by few.

c) Success focuses attention on the external. Excellence beams its spotlight on the internal, because excellence produces character.

d) Finally, success encourages expedience and compromise, which causes us to treat people as a means to an end. Excellence, on the other hand, cultivates principles and consistency.

Whatsoever thy hand findeth to do, do it with thy might; for there is no work, nor device, nor knowledge, nor wisdom, in the grave, whither thou goest.

Ecclesiastes 9:10 (KJV)

Give every assignment in your life your best effort. Practice excellence with your ministry. Always look for opportunities to go beyond average. Don't have a "thank God it's Friday" mentality. Can you imagine if your car, your food, or your dress was made by someone with this mentality? "Well, it's Friday and I've got to run home." Give everything you do your best effort.

Avoid Shortcuts

Whenever you take shortcuts in life, you only short cut yourself. Why? You deprive yourself of the impartation that is intended for you out of the process of excellence. You end up paying, whether you are a company that is producing something and has to recall a product, or you pay through a lawsuit, if you are an individual. The practice of excellence produces and releases impartations. Value excellence in your life, and one day it will show forth in the lives of those around you. You cannot simply teach excellence; you have to demonstrate it. People only catch what catches you. If it does not catch you, it will not catch anyone around you. You cannot mouth it, because if it has not been practiced, it will not have much effect.

Forasmuch as an excellent spirit, and knowledge, and understanding, interpreting of dreams, and showing of hard sentences, and dissolving of doubts, were found in the same Daniel, whom the king named Belteshazzar: now let Daniel be called, and he will show the interpretation.

Then was Daniel brought in before the king. And the king spake and said unto Daniel, Art thou that Daniel, which art of the children of the captivity of Judah, whom the king my father brought out of Jewry?

I have even heard of thee, that the spirit of the gods is in thee, and that light and understanding and excellent wisdom is found in thee.

Daniel 5:12-14 (KJV)

Don't settle for average or mediocre in life. Mediocrity means 'halfway up the mountain." It means partial achievement. We have half-achievement Christians and half-achievement work ethics. The mediocre route is always crowded and filled with union members. You don't have to be mediocre. When you get above average in life, people will quickly notice you. The King of Babylon picked Daniel because of the spirit of excellence in him. Excellence was found in everything Daniel did. You have to understand the background of Daniel. He was in Babylon in captivity. Life was throwing him a curveball. He was not being paid well. He had no medical benefits. He was a slave. He was a minority guy from another nation. Yet the King of Babylon picked Daniel because he saw the oil of excellence on him in everything Daniel did. The oil of excellence on you, your ministry, and your marriage will cause you or your ministry or marriage to stand out in a crowd. It will draw divine attention to you, and like Daniel, it will promote you.

I have even heard of thee, that the spirit of the gods is in thee, and that light and understanding and excellent wisdom is found in thee.

Daniel 5:14 (KJV)

It pleased Darius to set over the kingdom an hundred and twenty princes, which should be over the whole kingdom;

Daniel 6:1 (KJV)

Good news travels fast in the land of average and mediocre. Notice what distinguished Daniel from the others. It was not his bank account. It was not his permed hair. It was not because he knew the pastor. It was not his suit or his race. It was the very oil of excellence on him that promoted him, that distinguished him, and that set him apart from the sloppy and average bunch in Babylon.

It does not matter what life has thrown at you. An excellent spirit will carry you above it and into the attention of other people. It just takes a little bit more. Conformity is the shortest distance to acceptance in a crowd. People will always congregate with the crowds. You will never find creativity in a crowd. You will never find excellence in a crowd. It is an individual's effort. And they are so few who are willing to walk in it, that when you walk in it, it will set you apart and above the crowd.

Obtaining Excellence

Excellence can be obtained if you (i) care more than others think is wise; (ii) risk more than others think is safe; (iii) dream more than others think is practical; (iv) expect more than others think is possible; and (v) work more than others think is necessary.

The righteous is more excellent than his neighbour:
but the way of the wicked seduceth them.

Proverbs 12:26 (KJV)

The Scripture says that the righteous man ought to be more excellent than his neighbor. That is the expectation of God. This is sometimes hard to prove if your yard looks like a weed patch, and you drive around town with a broken muffler dragging beneath a bumper sticker that reads "Jesus Heals, Delivers and Prosperity is For Me." Determine in your life not to settle for average or mediocre. Pursue excellence in ministry and in your life and it will put you over.

CHAPTER III

ETHICS AND INTEGRITY

And as for me, You have upheld me in my integrity and set me in Your presence forever.

Psalm 41:12 (AMP)

The integrity of the upright shall guide them, but the willful contrariness *and* crookedness of the treacherous shall destroy them.

Proverb 11:3 (AMP)

Let integrity and uprightness preserve me; for I wait on thee.

Psalms 25:21 (KJV)

To achieve and grow in excellence, you must possess ethics and integrity. The Scripture says that God will uphold me in my integrity. Whether you are being sued or being challenged, if you did not cheat, and you did it right to the best of your knowledge, God says, "Relax. I will uphold you in your integrity." Integrity is one of our warfare resources. It is a shield of protection when it is used.

Hereafter I will not talk much with you: for the prince of this world cometh, and hath nothing in me.

John 14:30 (KJV)

The word "ethics" means a rule or a system of conduct that governs your life. For you to grow in excellence in life and in ministry, you must have principles or rules of conduct that govern your life as a believer, and you must determine to practice them. Jesus said, "the enemy comes, but he has nothing on me." That is integrity talking. If you are going to walk in excellence and see the promotion of the Lord, you must make ethics and integrity your personal friend.

Attending to Details

Pay attention to details in your life. People of excellence understand the importance of everything working right. They see the big picture, but they do not neglect the small details. They realize that a small leak can eventually sink a great ship. They realize that it takes a small, unattended leak in a church, in a marriage, in a ministry and in your life to sink your ship, no matter how great it is. Excellence means doing your best in everything, every time, and in every way. It means doing things right the first time. Our goal should be to be the best that we can be. Stu Leonard, the owner of the world's largest dairy store said, "First, we will be the best. Then we will be the first." In other words, you are not going to be the first long, if you are not the best. Your goal should not be to be the first. Your goal should be to be the best in what you are doing. By being the best, and being excellent, you receive the blessing of elevation in your area of pursuit.

When Michelangelo was painting the ceiling of the Sistine Chapel in Rome, he was painting in an obscure upper corner in the building that could not be seen from the floor below. One of his friends came to visit him and wondered why Michelangelo was concentrating so much effort on an obscure part of the painting that no one would see. Michelangelo's response was that even though no one sees it, God will see it. He said, "I am not painting for the Pope. I am painting this for God." When you adopt and maintain this kind of attitude of excellence in your work, ministry, marriage, and in all your responsibilities, you will see doors of promotion and opportunities come your way. Sometimes we are tempted to have a "get by with what will be accepted" philosophy, and we wonder why promotion is not coming our way.

How to Begin the Practice of Integrity in Your Life

First, establish boundaries of integrity in your life. Boundaries of integrity determine what you will and will not do, the places you will and will not go, the things you will and will not say, and the things you will and will not watch. Establish for yourself the "forbidden fruit" that you will never eat, despite the temptation.

Second, determine to walk in character. Your personal quest for excellence is another way of saying that your character is showing. That is, the day you decide to make excellence your priority, that is the beginning of a new demand that will be placed on your character. Excellence and character walk hand in hand. You cannot walk in excellence without walking in character.

The character of your business, your marriage, and your character as a believer is the sum total of the character of the church you attend. If you give your word, keep it. If you promise to do something, do it, not in the next millennium. That is character. The problem is that some of us never had people in our lives who demanded it. That is why you have in most churches people who want to come in late to services, who don't want to tithe, or be a part of church life, and yet want promotion from God. Then, when you discipline them, they say "I'm out of here. There's no love in this place." Or, "They're trying to control me."

Talent Versus Faithfulness

A talebearer revealeth secrets: but he that is of a faithful spirit concealeth the matter.

Proverbs 11:13 (KJV)

Most men will proclaim every one his own goodness: but a faithful man who can find?

Proverbs 20:6 (KJV)

Talent is not a rare commodity. It is very easy to find talented people. We have incredible talent in this nation and in the body of Christ. You can buy and hire talent anywhere, if you want it. What is rare are faithful people of character.

The Scripture says that a faithful man is difficult to find, and that faithful people know how to conceal a matter. Talented people are not hard to find. Put an advert out and you will find throngs of them at your door steps. What makes you valuable to a ministry, to a church, a leader, an employer or a friend is not your talent. It is your character and your faithfulness to them.

When you have an individual who has an incredible talent, he or she did nothing to earn it. He was born with it. So what is the reward? Why should I reward an individual who never paid the price for what they own? How many of us know that when we got baptized in the Holy Spirit, He did not make us tell the truth or make us faithful. This comes through character and discipline. You have to develop that discipline yourself. You have to demand that with a penalty in your life, or it will not get done.

Rewarding Faithfulness

Thou therefore, my son, be strong in the grace that is in Christ Jesus.

2 Timothy 2:1 (KJV)

And the things that thou hast heard of me among many witnesses, the same commit thou to faithful men, who shall be able to teach others also.

2 Timothy 2:2 (KJV)

We must put value on individuals who are faithful, committed, loyal, who keep rank and walk in excellence. I am going to take someone who is less talented, but who is faithful and has excellence in spirit, because you can always count on them. The problem with the church is that we have allowed gifted people, because of their talent and abilities, to get by and to intimidate other people with their bad behavior. The church ends up harboring these rebellious, divisive and destructive people who, with their bad behavior, run the house of God. Because of their talent and abilities, the church is afraid to lose them. Eventually, it becomes a disaster for the other team players or members who want to work together, walk in excellence and accomplish the vision of the house. A wise leader who is concerned about the whole picture, will eventually get rid of those individuals for the sake of the vision. Leaders must learn to honor and reward character over gifting. Reward those around you who are faithful, who have character, and who walk in excellence, not those who have gifting and are unreliable and uncommitted.

There was an article written about a firm in St. Louis, Missouri that was downsizing and laying off twenty percent of its workforce. The company managers decided to devise a strategy of who to lay off, and who to keep on board. They decided they would keep those of high moral character – not the most talented people, but those who had been faithful, committed, and who had helped to build the company. They would get rid of those with talent, because those with talent can always be replaced. However, committed, faithful people are rare and difficult to replace.

CHAPTER IV

GOING THE EXTRA MILE

Ye have heard that it hath been said, An eye for an eye, and a tooth for a tooth:

But I say unto you, That ye resist not evil: but whosoever shall smite thee on thy right cheek, turn to him the other also.

And if any man will sue thee at the law, and take away thy coat, let him have thy cloak also.

And whosoever shall compel thee to go a mile, go with him twain.

Give to him that asketh thee, and from him that would borrow of thee turn not thou away.

Matthew 5:38-42 (KJV)

Going the extra mile is an important principle to achieving and maintaining excellence in ministry, in marriage, in a job and in our individual lives. Always be prepared to go the extra mile. If you are not someone who loves to go the extra mile, you will not be able to develop a spirit of excellence in your life and ministry. Excellence is meant for people who are willing to go beyond the call of duty, who are willing to work and to pay the price.

In Matthew chapter five, Jesus began to deal with the principle of the extra mile. Jesus taught a non-resistance to going the extra mile, to going beyond average. He dealt with this principle from three perspectives. The first way we are forced to practice the extra mile principle in Matthew chapter five is learning to go beyond revenging what has been done to you. The second way is going beyond litigation, and the third way is becoming unlimited in your rendering of service. You cannot be a 9:00 a.m. to 5:00 p.m. individual when it comes to kingdom life, if you are going to maintain a life of excellence. Excellence demands going the extra mile. Don't ever be afraid to give your best to what seems to be a small task, because each time you conquer one small task, it makes you stronger. When you do the little jobs well, the big ones tend to take care of themselves. In Luke 16:10, Jesus said he that is faithful in little, I will make him ruler over much.

A Picture of the Extra Mile Principle

And he made his camels to kneel down without the city by a well of water at the time of the evening, even the time that women go out to draw water.

And he said, O LORD God of my master Abraham, I pray thee, send me good speed this day, and show kindness unto my master Abraham.

Behold, I stand here by the well of water; and the daughters of the men of the city come out to draw water:

And let it come to pass, that the damsel to whom I shall say, Let down thy pitcher, I pray thee, that I may drink; and she shall say, Drink, and I will give thy camels drink also: let the same be she that thou hast appointed for thy servant Isaac; and thereby shall I know that thou hast showed kindness unto my master.

And it came to pass, before he had done speaking, that, behold, Rebekah came out, who was born to Bethuel, son of Milcah, the wife of Nahor, Abraham's brother, with her pitcher upon her shoulder.

And the damsel was very fair to look upon, a virgin, neither had any man known her: and she went down to the well, and filled her pitcher, and came up.

And the servant ran to meet her, and said, Let me, I pray thee, drink a little water of thy pitcher.

And she said, Drink, my lord: and she hasted, and let down her pitcher upon her hand, and gave him drink.

And when she had done giving him drink, she said, I will draw water for thy camels also, until they have done drinking.

**And she hasted, and emptied her pitcher into the
trough, and ran again unto the well to draw water,
and drew for all his camels.**

Genesis 24:11-20 (KJV)

This is the story of Abraham sending his servant to get a
bride for his only son, Isaac. In biblical typology, it is the
picture of God the Father sending the Holy Spirit to get a
bride (the Church) for His only begotten Son, Jesus. This is
a natural shadow of that in the old covenant. The question is,
when the servant goes to look for a bride for Isaac, what are
the criteria he is looking for, in order to know which woman
to choose? At sundown, the servant knew the wells were
crowded with maidens. He knew the criteria was not her bust
measurement, length of her hair, her beauty, the way she
walks or the color of her skin.

The servant prayed a prayer that actually revealed one of
God's criteria. He prayed that "she may not only offer me a
drink of water, but my camels also." The servant knew that
all the maidens would not be willing to draw water for his ten
camels. He knew that was not going to happen in their
culture. In the midst of the crowd at the well, there was a little

maiden called Rebekah who came to the servant willing to offer him and his camels a drink of water.

Often, when we read Genesis 24, we tend to overlook the importance of what Rebekah did. First of all, we must understand that there were ten camels. Second, they had just traveled five hundred miles. Third, each of the camels can drink forty gallons. That is four hundred gallons of water. Fourth, Rebekah was about fourteen years old. She had no pump, and no hose. She had only a pitcher or jar to draw water from the well. This was not an attractive assignment, and not all the women would be willing to do this.

The Right Attitudes

In Genesis 24, there were three principles that were found in the prayer that the servant prayed, and all of the principles deal with the attitude of Rebekah. The first thing that the servant prayed was that God would help him find someone who is willing to inconvenience herself for someone else. Second, he prayed that God would provide someone who is willing to forget her own, in order to please someone else. Finally, he prayed for someone who is willing and able to make a difference in the life of Isaac. Rebekah's response to the servant was, "I am going to make a difference in your life. I am going to inconvenience myself for the next four hours, so that I can make a difference in your life." Rebekah had no idea what her return was going to be for the extra effort.

For I say unto you, That except your righteousness shall exceed the righteousness of the scribes and Pharisees, ye shall in no case enter into the kingdom of heaven.

Matthew 5:20 (KJV)

The Scripture makes it more clear. Our righteousness must exceed that of the Pharisees in order to see the kingdom of God. What Jesus is saying is that, unless what we do goes further, unless it goes beyond what you are paid to do, or forced to do, or asked to do, or made to do, unless your whole life, your spirit and your outlook exceeds the righteousness of the scribes and Pharisees, you cannot see the kingdom of heaven.

Lessons From Rebekah's Life

The life of Rebekah teaches us two important lessons:

(1)   We are not to live our lives as legalists. That is, we must not allow our lives to go by the rule books, if we are going to achieve the spirit of excellence in our lives, marriages, and ministries. Always go beyond the rule books. Losers and those who are mediocre in life play only by the time clock. Average people always make sure they never give more than is expected or demanded of them. If you are really giving to life – whether in marriage, in a job, in ministry or in relationships more than you receive, don't ever regret it. Somebody down the road will recognize it. You are only going to be remembered by two things in life: (i) the problems you helped solve; and (ii) the problems you caused or created. Ask yourself which one will you want to be remembered for. When you give more in your endeavors, you are building your future.

(2)   Extra blessings are a result of extra effort. That is a principle. There is no traffic jam on the freeway of the extra mile. Why? Because all of the average people exit after the first mile. When Rebekah watered the camels, she did not realize what she was about to embrace. She did not know that on those camels was all of the gold, silver, jewelry and linens that were gifts to her from a wealthy father who was looking to select a bride for his son. She did not even know that what she was doing was going to put her in the ancestral line of Jesus Christ the Messiah. She was going to become the great-great-great-great-great-great-great-great-great-great-great-great-great-grandmother of the coming Messiah.

The Distinguishing Factor

What was it that distinguished Rebekah from the others? It was not her perm, her beauty, or her 18 karat gold cross around her neck. She went beyond average. She went beyond the expectations of others. She crossed the mediocre line.

Normally, when you do, you will stand out in a group, in a church, in a leadership team, and in a job.

In practicing excellence, show genuine respect for others all the time. Why? Because people of excellence cannot achieve excellence alone. They need the assistance of other people. Don't devalue people. Elevate the worth of others to the same level you hold for yourself. Our actions must be genuine. You cannot make an individual feel important in your presence if you secretly feel he is a nobody. When we really feel that those we are working with are not on our level, what happens is that we leave the level of excellence, because we feel that it is not important and necessary for them.

CHAPTER V

DEVELOPING COMMITMENT FOR EXCELLENCE

Commitment is the ingredient to completing a task. It is the ingredient that every winner possesses. It is the key to excellence in your ministry, in marriage and in your life. Jesus said My meat is to do the will of the Father and to finish it. That is commitment. Commitment gives you the ability and tenacity to complete every task that you begin. You don't have to be a mediocre Christian. You can walk in excellence by being committed to everything you begin in life. The spirit of commitment in a Christian's life, in a ministry or in a marriage, will release the oil of excellence on their behalf.

What is commitment? Commitment means to join together, to bring together, to do with something or with somebody. Commitment is a God idea. You can never build anything significant and strong without the ingredient of commitment. Commitment builds. Anything that God builds has this at its base or its foundation. Commitment is covenant. When you commit to a thing, you are simply saying, whether consciously or unconsciously, that you are in covenant with that thing, marriage or business, church or friendship. In the Old Testament, the Hebrews, in showing their commitment one to another or to a thing, exchanged their belts that had their swords, daggers and weapons with one another. It is symbolic that anybody that touches you, touches me, and also that all of my abilities to fight are at your disposal. That is the essence of commitment. When you are committed to a thing, you receive these benefits. You receive the benefits, the blessings and the abilities that come from what you are committed to.

Characteristics of Commitment

Commitment is always active and not passive. Commitment is not simply existing in a thing without joining to that thing and participating in it. It is not simply existing in a thing. It is getting involved and contributing to a thing and making that thing more effective and better. You can be in a church and yet not be committed. You are in the church, yet you are lost. It looks like you took the wrong turn to a

Tupperware meeting, and don't know you are not in a Tupperware meeting. Commitment is being active. It is contributing to a thing. Sitting in church does not mean that you are committed to the life of the church. Living with your wife or your husband does not mean that you are committed to the marriage.

A commitment to your future and your destiny is not just going through life with the attitude "if it happens, it happens." It is actively pursuing the will of God for your life, even when it seems impossible. Commitment is not just showing up. It is sowing your life into something. Vince Lombardi said that "the quality of a man's life is in direct proportion to his commitment regardless of his career."

The second characteristic of commitment is that genuine commitment is affirmed. When it comes to something you believe in, recognize the power of the spoken word and commit yourself to it. If our words are supposed to be our bond, then when you give it, you commit yourself to it. When you are taking a marriage vow, you say "I do." When you say that, not only have you become committed, but you have sealed that commitment with the power of your word. Your word is supposed to put a seal on your commitment.

Third, genuine commitment is built out of relationship with God. You must build your commitment out of your relationship with God. Why? Because if you are serving the Lord and people let you down, you won't allow that to destroy your commitment to your spouse, your ministry or to your friendship.

Serve the LORD with gladness: come before his presence with singing.

Psalms 100:2 (KJV)

The Scripture says "serve the Lord with gladness." It is out of this attitude and spirit of gladness that you build the very commitment of your life. When you build your commitment out of your relationship with God, and when you get hurt, the first thing in your mind will not be to leave the church, leave your spouse, or to resign from your area of ministry.

Fourth, genuine commitment is not built from the law. It is built from grace. You don't build commitment from legalism. If it is legalism, it becomes hard. There will be struggles but the struggles make us better. "Well, I said that I'll marry her, even if it kills me." That is not commitment. Do you love her? Can you stay with her? Can you handle the rolls on her sides? Can you deal with the fake nails or fake eyelashes?

Commitment is building out of relationship, and not out of rules. When you love where you are, whether it is the church that God has placed you in, the men and women of God that God has placed over you, or the spouse that you are married to, you will be strongly committed. But if you don't, you will stay bitter, resentful and never be committed.

Commitment is motivated by love. If it is not love, you will not do it for the long haul. "I want to be faithful to her, not I have to be. I want to come to church, not I have to come. I want to help in this ministry, not I have to help." The law activates the power of sin. The law produces death. You cannot be a successful Christian out of the law. When you do, you will continually be a failure. Do you ever get tired of what you are committed to? Yes. But why do you stay committed to it? Because you are committed to the benefit of it.

Finally, genuine commitment swallows up all other options. If I make a commitment in marriage, in friendship, and to be involved in a church, there is no other option. Your first love, your first attention and faithfulness is to the one and the place you are committed to. Divorce and an extramarital affair are not an option in the marriage.

When you know that there is no other option in a thing because of your commitment to that thing or place, you always opt to resolve problems, instead of just walking out or retreating from that relationship or church.

The Attitudes of Committed People

Thou therefore, my son, be strong in the grace that is in Christ Jesus.

And the things that thou hast heard of me among many witnesses, the same commit thou to faithful men, who shall be able to teach others also.

Thou therefore endure hardness, as a good soldier of Jesus Christ.

No man that warreth entangleth himself with the affairs of this life; that he may please him who hath chosen him to be a soldier.

And if a man also strive for masteries, yet is he not crowned, except he strive lawfully.

The husbandman that laboureth must be first partaker of the fruits.

2 Timothy 2:1-6 (KJV)

Typically in the church we commit things to anointed people, talented people and gifted people who are not faithful nor committed to anything but their own desire, agenda and ambition. If a person is not faithful and committed to a thing, but merely able, there will be destruction in that thing. God wants us to find faithful men and He will make them able.

Thou therefore endure hardness, as a good soldier of Jesus Christ.

2 Timothy 2:3 (KJV)

The first attitude of commitment that will build power and produce benefit in your life is that it prepares you to endure hardship. In any relationship, whether with your spouse, your friend or in the church, you are going to face and experience some tough times, experiences, and some dry seasons. It happens to every believer. In sports, there is what you call a slump and that is when that individual is not functioning at his best or at what is expected of him. Normally, what is done with the athlete is that they have to go back to their fundamentals and work their way back up again.

That is true also in a relationship. When you experience a dry season, without commitment in your life, you will not be able to go through the hard time. The symbol of Christianity is the cross. It is an execution symbol. The evidence of a crucified life is your willingness to do His will and lay your will down.

The second attitude is that a committed person refuses to be entangled by the affairs of this life. The desire for fame, the desire for money and the desire for things can take you away from your commitment. If the devil cannot take you out with trouble, problems or afflictions, then he will try to take you out with success.

God wants us to have good success and He wants us to prosper. But God does not want our success to capture our hearts.

> **No man that warreth entangleth himself with the affairs of this life; that he may please him who hath chosen him to be a soldier.**
>
> **2 Timothy 2:4 (KJV)**

The third attitude is that a committed person is not concerned with pleasing himself. He lives to please the one who enlisted him in the army.

And if a man also strive for masteries, yet is he not crowned, except he strive lawfully.

2 Timothy 2:5 (KJV)

The fourth attitude is that a committed person has his eyes on the prize. The devil cannot kill you. You kill yourself with meaningless and purposeless living, that is, living life without a goal. Don't pursue what you are not called to pursue. Stay within the sphere of your prize. Focus on your prize.

And if a man also strive for masteries, yet is he not crowned, except he strive lawfully.

2 Timothy 2:5 (KJV)

The fifth attitude is that committed people compete according to the rules. When you got married, you said "I do." There are certain rules in the marriage that you must live by and committed people live by the rule set in the game.

Every place that the sole of your foot shall tread upon, that have I given unto you, as I said unto Moses.

From the wilderness and this Lebanon even unto the great river, the river Euphrates, all the land of the Hittites, and unto the great sea toward the going down of the sun, shall be your coast.

There shall not any man be able to stand before thee all the days of thy life: as I was with Moses, so I will be with thee: I will not fail thee, nor forsake thee.

Joshua 1:3-5 (KJV)

Boundaries protect our lives. You can see them as a limit or as a defense. When a boundary is set up early in life, it will protect you. You will be able to establish something in your life that you will never do – You won't steal. You won't rob a bank. You won't commit immorality – all because of the boundaries that you have set in your life. If you don't have this, you might end up losing your life, your family and ministry. You must compete according to the rules.

The husbandman that laboureth must be first partaker of the fruits.

2 Timothy 2:6 (KJV)

Finally, committed people know the power of hard work. Committed people are not afraid of hard work as a way of developing excellence. We don't work to go to heaven. Jesus already did that for us. But we work to have an excellent marriage, an excellent ministry and church. We work to have good relationships and to raise our children. It is tough.

Enemies of Commitment

When we make up our minds to commit to excellence, there are going to be some hindrances that we will encounter. These hindrances are the very enemies of commitment. Let's look at them.

Knowing this, that the trying of your faith worketh patience.

James 1:3 (KJV)

The **first** enemy is **painless faith**. There is no such thing as life without a challenge. Those who have believed the lies of painless faith draw back from the commitment to excellence when pain comes like it is a stranger. There is no painless faith. If you are going to walk in excellence, understand that you will be challenged. There will be challenges and opposition. Before any promotion there is always a test.

Your faith has to be tested and built so that, as God promotes you, what is inside of you is growing as the outside opposition is growing or you will collapse. We have seen and heard of ministries and churches all over the land that take off like a jet plane, then get to a certain altitude and blow up. Why? Because they did not grow inside as the outside opposition was growing. They did not grow in their faith and in their character. A gift is given, but fruit grows over a period of time.

You don't wake up, plant an apple tree and then expect it to produce fruit the next day. It takes years to grow. Yet you can have a gift and still be a fool, irresponsible, immature and full of selfish ambition. It is what is inside of you that holds you as the gifts in you begin to gain altitude.

The **second** enemy of commitment is **the personality pitfall**. Your personality can be a gift from God or it can be a curse. It depends on how you allow it to dominate you. We are all different. We have our strength and our weakness. Determine to work on your weakness because it can take you away from commitment.

> **Let this mind be in you, which was also in Christ Jesus:**
>
> **Philippians 2:5 (KJV)**

Jesus said let this mind be in you. What mind? The same mind and the same attitude that Jesus had about everything should be in us. Take on the same thinking as Christ, and where your personality works against the purpose of God, work on it.

The **third** enemy of commitment to excellence is **short-term thinking.** It destroys commitment quickly. When you feel that you will only be in a relationship, in a church or in a business for a short while, you will never be committed to pursue excellence in everything you do. Instead, you will be a parasite always sucking and not giving. There is a common phrase used in the church world that shows lack of commitment – "I am only here for a season." "I am just waiting for Him to direct me to my next assignment." Or, the Jesus-is-coming-in-six-weeks mentality. You can never be committed to a thing, if you have short-term thinking.

The Ultimate Commitment

Jesus made the ultimate commitment. He committed His life to God. Notice three things that happened in these verses of Scripture.

> **And he was withdrawn from them about a stone's cast, and kneeled down, and prayed,**
>
> **Luke 22:41 (KJV)**

He withdrew a stone's throw from His disciples. With Jesus, the power of His commitment to Father took Him away from His disciples. It may take you away from some people. If you are going to be committed to pursue excellence in a thing, you will find yourself being taken away from some things. That is part of the deal.

> **Saying, Father, if thou be willing, remove this cup from me: nevertheless not my will, but thine, be done.**
>
> **Luke 22:42 (KJV)**

Second, Jesus said that if there is any other way, please tell me quickly. Unfortunately, there was no other way, so He said "Nevertheless not My will, but Your will be done." That is the evidence of the crucified life. What is the lesson here? The lesson is that Jesus laid His will down to commit to the will of another – the Father.

> **And there appeared an angel unto him from heaven, strengthening him.**
>
> **Luke 22:43 (KJV)**

Third, immediately an angel of the Lord appeared to strengthen Jesus. Many people never experience the strength of the Lord because they never make a total commitment to pursue something. The strength and grace comes after commitment is made.

The fourth enemy is broken focus. Focus is very important to commitment. You will always discern your level of commitment by your level of focus. Once the enemy can break your focus, he has tampered with your commitment to God, to a place, to things and even to people. Every time people are not committed, check their focus. You will find that whatever they are focusing on is what they are committed to.

WHAT COMMITMENT WORKS IN YOUR LIFE

Let us look at some of the things that the power of commitment will build in your life. Commitment has great benefits. When you make up your mind to walk in the spirit of commitment, there will be a release of these benefits in your life.

The **first** thing commitment will release in your life is **the power of accomplishment.** Most Christians don't accomplish anything in their lives. They live life like tumbleweeds. Jesus committed His entire life to the will of the Father.

Because He was willing to lay down His life, He was able to declare at the end of it, "Father, I have finished the work that You gave Me to do." On the cross He cried out with a loud voice, not a wimpy voice, and He said "It is finished." In the Hebrew, it means *totalista* – that is, "paid in full." In other words, "I did not take a shortcut. I stayed on course, and I finished well." If we are part of His family, and we have His DNA in us, then why don't we like to be committed to anything? When the show was over with Jesus Christ, there was a sense of accomplishment that came with His commitment to the Father's will.

The Apostle Paul at the end of his ministry felt this sense of accomplishment. He said "I have kept the faith. I have fought a good fight. I have finished my course." But to get to that point, he was shipwrecked, beaten up, jailed and stoned, and many people forsook him. He said at the end of his life "only Luke is with me." Demas forsook him. Most of the guys that started with him did not remain with him. They bailed out. Not being able to be committed to a thing or a place is a sign of weak character, immaturity, and a lack of tenacity, and an inability to see something through.

Wisdom has built her house, She has hewn out her seven pillars;

Proverbs 9:1 (NAS)

The **second** thing commitment will release into your life is **the power to build.** The Scripture says that "wisdom has built her house." I wish that it said power or spiritual gifts have built the house, but it says that wisdom has built the house.

If you live in the wisdom of God, you will know the power of commitment which will build the purposes of God. Most people don't know the power of commitment because they do not live in the wisdom of God, and so they cannot see the purposes of God built. Nothing happens overnight in regard to your future and mine and our destiny. It is not a short-term quick fix thing. The purpose of God is to be built into my life, and that takes a long time and is a long process.

Usually when we see somebody that we really admire and like, we skip what they have been through that got them there. We admire their ministry and want to be like them, but you do not know what happened to them when they were twenty-seven years old. You don't know the tragedy that happened in their life. You don't know the hurt and pain, and the many nights of not sleeping. They got to where they are right now over a process of time.

Wisdom always builds God's purposes in your life. And the wisdom of God is to have the spirit of commitment that holds on and sees the things that you have committed yourself to finish. If there is no commitment, you are always starting over again, always rebuilding. So take the commitment to study, to grow, to learn, and to build something in your life and commit yourself to it and see it through.

> **Not forsaking the assembling of ourselves together, as the manner of some is; but exhorting one another: and so much the more, as ye see the day approaching.**
>
> **Hebrews 10:25 (KJV)**

The **third** thing that commitment will build in your life is **the power of belonging**. Commitment will build into your life the power of belonging. Don't easily give up on gathering together with other believers. It is not an option. It is a commitment. And when someone has the spirit of commitment in a family or in a local church, they receive the power of belonging. Have you ever heard of people who died, they decomposed, and three months later somebody found them in the house because of the body odor? They had been dead for three months and nobody missed them. The only way they found out was because of the odor. That is bad for a person who can decompose and nobody misses them for three months.

Some Christians don't have friends. They are loners. You know why? Because they don't want to commit to someone to be their friend. The Bible says that he who wants a friend must make himself friendly. If you don't have a friend, that is because you are not willing to commit to anything. You want everybody to commit to you, but you don't want to commit to anybody.

Two are better than one, because they have a good return for their work:

If one falls down, his friend can help him up. But pity the man who falls and has no one to help him up!

Ecclesiastes 4:9-10 (NIV)

Commitment ties other people into your life and when other people come into your life, the two of you become better than when you were just one. If you go into a city to visit, and I am tied in with other men of God in that area, I am able to recommend you to them. And they will treat you well, not because you are very good but because of the commitment they have to me, and me to them.

Favor and opportunities come out of relationships. You are going to miss your destiny if you cannot maintain commitment, if you cannot maintain tying into other people's lives, staying the course, and sowing into them on good days and bad days. If you don't sow into a church, if you don't put in your life, your time, your family and your money, your heart will not be in the church. Where your treasure is, that is where your heart is – in your car, in your golf bag. Committed people always have a lot of friends who care.

The **next** thing that commitment releases in you is **the power of ownership**. When you are committed to your church, to a purpose and to a vision, you can say it is my church, it is my vision. We become a people of one spirit and it comes out of our commitment.

The **fifth** thing that is released out of commitment is **the power of prosperity and success**. Prosperity will not drift over you like a cloud. It comes from the fruit of commitment.

> **This book of the law shall not depart out of thy mouth; but thou shalt meditate therein day and night, that thou mayest observe to do according to all that is written therein: for then thou shalt make thy way prosperous, and then thou shalt have good success.**
>
> **Joshua 1:8 (KJV)**

God told Joshua that if he is going to make his way prosperous, he will have to meditate on some things. Meditation takes commitment. It takes focus. What do you mediate on? Check what you meditate on and you will find out why you are not prospering in certain areas – are you still meditating on your ex-boyfriend or ex-husband? What do you meditate on? Meditation helps to expand our minds. It brings to earth what heaven already possesses.

The shark is very popular with aquarium owners. The reason is that the shark will never grow beyond the environment that you put it in. The shark will not get bigger than the aquarium (its environment), but if you take the same 5-inch shark and put it in an ocean, that shark will grow to 8-feet. Like the shark, we are made for the ocean.

> **He becometh poor that dealeth with a slack hand:**
> **but the hand of the diligent maketh rich.**
>
> **Proverbs 10:4 (KJV)**

How much better is it to get wisdom than gold!
and to get understanding rather to be chosen
than silver!

Proverbs 16:16 (KJV)

Receive my instruction, and not silver; and
knowledge rather than choice gold.

Proverbs 8:10 (KJV)

My people are destroyed for lack of knowledge:
because thou hast rejected knowledge, I will
also reject thee, that thou shalt be no priest to
me: seeing thou hast forgotten the law of thy
God, I will also forget thy children.

Hosea 4:6 (KJV)

The **sixth** thing that is released from commitment is
the power of knowledge. The power of knowledge is
released to those who are committed. Receiving
knowledge comes out of our commitment of wanting it
badly. Sometimes you have to dig for it. Knowledge is
power. If you are committed to growing and learning,

you gain the power of knowledge which will release you from mediocrity and bring excellence to you.

Commitment to growing and learning will slap the ugly butt of mediocrity. People live way below their potential because they have never put in the kind of commitment that builds the kind of knowledge that releases the purposes of God.

> **According as his divine power hath given unto us all things that pertain unto life and godliness, through the knowledge of him that hath called us to glory and virtue:**
>
> **2 Peter 1:3 (KJV)**

A commitment to grow and to learn can cause you to live under the power of knowledge. It is the knowledge of Christ that brings you all things pertaining to life and godliness. Every one of the purposes of God can be released into your life.

CHAPTER VI

CONSISTENCY IN GROWTH

Developing consistency in our lives is a key factor to growing and achieving excellence. Be consistent in what you do. People will forget how fast you did a job, but they will always remember how well you did a job. A lot of people can be good for a moment. They can be excellent for a special event. However, only a few can do it day in and day out, with a consistently high level of performance. A twenty million dollar company is only as good as the five dollar an hour employee at the front desk.

You must never stop growing. Never stop growing and improving. Be consistent in your growth. Pat Riley, the head coach of the Miami Heat basketball team in one of his books wrote that "excellence is the gradual result of always striving to do better." People of excellence are always people of growth. There is no plateau, no stopping place. It is consistent improvement. What is excellent today, may not be excellent tomorrow. You must determine to keep growing. You must be flexible to new improvement. Keep learning, reading books, listening to tapes, and hanging around people who can improve you in every area, if you are going to achieve excellence in ministry and in your life. You cannot do it by just sitting on your rear end. You have to spend time in prayer, study the Word, hang around successful people, and even be willing to spend some money to improve your weakness. You are what you are by choice. Excellence is not how much you have in the bank. It is what you do with what you have.

Improvement Insight

Let us look at some of the ways to improve areas of our lives to walk in excellence.

❏ The first improvement insight is that self-improvement is the quality of a leader and not a follower. Self-improvement is the only way to remain in leadership. Standards of excellence are not set in stone. They are constantly being redefined. As we grow in life, as opportunities come, and as our income increases, God expects our level of excellence to rise correspondingly.

☐ Our greatest challenge is not gaining on others, or to outdo others, but to grow oneself. Determine to outdo your own yesterday. Your goal is to beat yourself, and not to keep up with somebody else. We are not equal. We are equal in relationship and in the love of God, but we are not equally gifted and talented.

Your goal should not be to compare yourself to anyone else, or any other church. Your goal should be to beat your personal best. What is your best? Your best is found in your potential. How do you do that? By getting someone better than you in front of you. When you find someone like that, run with them, hang with them, and see a difference in your life. Never coast on your past achievements. Constantly seek to improve and better your own standard.

❑ Finally, take responsibility for your own improvement. The failure to hit the bull's-eye is never the fault of the target. To improve your aim, improve yourself. You don't move the target. You move the gun.

The Four Types of People in Life

Always give a hundred and ten percent in everything you do. The difference between ordinary and extraordinary is a little extra. There are four types of people you will encounter in the areas of commitment and excellence.

❑ *Cop-out type*. They set no goals, and they make no decisions.

❑ *Hold out type*. This group of people is always uncertain if they can reach their goals, so they don't even start. They have self-esteem problems. They will give you twenty reasons why they cannot meet their goals. They have a "grasshopper" mentality – they are small in their own eyes.

**Jesus saith unto them, My meat is to do the will
of him that sent me, and to finish his work.**

John 4:34 (KJV)

❑ *Drop out type*. These types of people start,
but stop when it gets tough. They live their
lives with various uncompleted assignments.
Jesus says, "My meat is to do the will of the
Father and to finish it." Jesus was not a drop
out. He completed His assignment. We must
learn to do the same in our lives. Learn to
complete everything you begin. Demand it
from your children and your leaders.

❑ *All out type*. The final type is the "all out."
These groups set goals, pay the price, and
reach their objectives.

What type are you? Ask yourself these questions and
listen seriously to the answers from your own heart:

a. What do you really want in life?

b. What is it going to cost to attain it?

c. Am I willing to pay the price to attain what I really want?

d. When do I start paying the price?

No Installment Plan

And he said to them all, If any man will come after me, let him deny himself, and take up his cross daily, and follow me.

For whosoever will save his life shall lose it: but whosoever will lose his life for my sake, the same shall save it.

And it came to pass, that, as they went in the way, a certain man said unto him, Lord, I will follow thee whithersoever thou goest.

And Jesus said unto him, Foxes have holes, and birds of the air have nests; but the Son of man hath not where to lay his head.

And he said unto another, Follow me. But he said, Lord, suffer me first to go and bury my father.

Jesus said unto him, Let the dead bury their dead: but go thou and preach the kingdom of God.

Luke 9:23-24, 57-60 (KJV)

You don't pay for excellence on an installment plan. You pay more than you receive up front. Before you examine and experience the product, you pay for it. Then it begins to compound. Jesus always puts the cost and the Cross up front. He says, you cannot be My disciple unless you pick up your cross and are willing to pay the cost, and deny yourself. Jesus was not looking for a crowd. He was just looking for a few good men. He can change the world with a few good men of excellence. Nobody will listen to a crowd of mediocre people.

Determine to make excellence a lifestyle. Do things right the first time. It costs more to do it the second time. The quality of a person's life is in direct proportion to their level of commitment to excellence, regardless of their chosen field of endeavor. You don't just become great one day in the future. You become great starting today, by doing the right things today, and you will reap a great destiny tomorrow. Put yourself in a position for God to promote you. Demand it of yourself, and the people around you. Dare to rise above average. Dare to go the second mile. Teach it to your children. Model it before your employees, and it will pay rich eternal dividends.

To request a complete catalog featuring books, video or audio tapes by Dr. John A. Tetsola, or to contact him for speaking engagements, please write or call:

Ecclesia Word Ministries International
P.O. Box 743
Bronx, New York 10462

(718) 904-8530
(718) 904-8107 fax
www.ecclesiaword.org
www.reformersministries.org
email: reformers@msn.com